QUIET MIND,
OPEN HEART

Jade Black

BALBOA.
PRESS
A DIVISION OF HAY HOUSE

Balboa Press books may be ordered through booksellers or by contacting:

Balboa Press
A Division of Hay House
1663 Liberty Drive
Bloomington, IN 47403
www.balboapress.com
1 (877) 407-4847

Because of the dynamic nature of the Internet, any web addresses or
links contained in this book may have changed since publication and
may no longer be valid. The views expressed in this work are solely those
of the author and do not necessarily reflect the views of the publisher,
and the publisher hereby disclaims any responsibility for them.

The author of this book does not dispense medical advice or prescribe the use
of any technique as a form of treatment for physical, emotional, or medical
problems without the advice of a physician, either directly or indirectly. The
intent of the author is only to offer information of a general nature to help
you in your quest for emotional and spiritual well-being. In the event you use
any of the information in this book for yourself, which is your constitutional
right, the author and the publisher assume no responsibility for your actions.

Any people depicted in stock imagery provided by Thinkstock are
models, and such images are being used for illustrative purposes only.
Certain stock imagery © Thinkstock.

Printed in the United States of America.

ISBN: 978-1-4525-2264-7 (sc)
ISBN: 978-1-4525-2265-4 (e)

Library of Congress Control Number: 2014916831

Balboa Press rev. date: 10/2/2014

For Joshua, Dee, and Erin.
Your love endures the winds of change.

Contents

Introduction

The title of this book encompasses the two most important ventures of my life thus far. I believe they are the two most important ventures in everyone's life, but I wish to leave others' life objectives to them. It sounds so simple: just have an open heart and a quiet mind. With these two elements, you can experience the joy that you were meant to. To me, nothing else really matters; only God or pure loving awareness can provide this. This loving awareness, or God as I wish to refer to it, guides me to keep an open heart and a quiet, assured mind. I am only convinced of this because I've tried next to everything else to feel good about my life and my personal circumstances. All of my alternate attempts left me feeling only temporarily fulfilled, and soon enough I felt as if I hadn't moved at all. Nothing has fed me the way my relationship with God has. Nothing has washed me from the inside out like God's love, and I know that that will remain a truth close to my heart as I move forward.

Anyone who has tried to transition from negative to positive thinking knows how hard it is. At first it takes effort—a lot of effort. Negative, angry, and judgmental thoughts about everything used to rule my life. I was once one of the angriest people I'd ever known, and somehow being angry felt almost good. It felt like home. It only felt like home because it was my default, and I had nothing else to compare it to. I often thought to myself that it was just the way life was. It's not.

If there was a cynical thought in the universe, I abused it until desolation. Learning to quiet the mind is developed through various practices, all of which are helpful. Some people meditate, pray, work various psychological programs, or gain understanding to quiet their minds. All of those are great, and all of those can be rather trapping. What I mean by "trapping" is that we sometimes get stuck in those methods and fail to move freely to others. Opening up to all methods, or taking what we need from several practices, results in a type of worldliness. It results in a deeper understanding of ourselves and the social world we encounter every day.

When I first began my spiritual journey I was riddled with thoughts about my methods, and that later became a burden in itself. *Am I doing it right? Is this working? When will I become enlightened? When will I encounter sheer joy and peace? Should I be doing more psychotherapy?* I've found that the answers to those questions are rather futile. I often heard God whisper to me in the still of my day, "Just try loving who you are. See yourself the way I see you." It really is that simple. There is no one solution to anything. There is nothing to figure out. All we have to do is let it go. Sure analytical people such as myself strive to really "get it," but in the end none of that matters. All that matters is that you let it go.

I have found that applying the kindness, patience, and love toward myself the way God does toward all of us is helpful. It makes me smile to think that I am able to be kind to myself in such a way. In turn, by being kind to myself, I automatically become more kind toward others.

Maintaining an open heart is another task in itself. I've struggled with keeping my heart open. I found it hardest to love those who I felt had wronged me. The fact is that no person or event has wronged me, and every person I've encountered and have yet to encounter is innocent. I believe that every person is filled with love. I truly believe that even the most hated people on earth, those who have caused others tremendous suffering, are still pure love. They may not know it, they may not practice it, but underneath every behavior is a soul that prides itself on love.

Throughout my spiritual journey I have worked quite hard at forgiveness for others and myself. There are many definitions of forgiveness, but to me it represents peace over an event that once elicited negative feelings. Through developing forgiveness for myself, I have learned to extend that toward others. Forgiveness now comes far more easily than before, and it feels amazing to see God in every person, including myself, for God is love.

My dog has been instrumental in helping me keep my heart open. I've always had a special connection with animals. Perhaps it's their ability to be mindful and unconditional in love, but I know that when I quickly try to close my heart my dog can open it just as quickly.

Beyond my dog being a teacher of devotion, God has taught me that keeping my heart open is essential to fulfilling His plan and impacting others in a positive way. In my experience, nothing changes a seemingly negative situation the way pure, open hearts do.

So I suppose it seems easy. You may think that I'm offering a simple solution for all of life's problems, and I guess I sort of am. But getting to a place where we can keep open hearts through everything takes courage, faith, and trust. It took me reflecting on my past and diving into how I felt about everything that I have experienced. I asked myself why I felt a certain way about those who I felt had harmed me, and it came back to one thing: lack of love. Real or perceived, I believed I did not deserve love from myself or anyone else. This is the basis of this book. In order to appropriately illustrate this process I have so pleasantly experienced, I have to first discuss some personal elements of my life and how I was able to change my perception of their purpose.

CHAPTER 1

Hopeless

I saw my olive DKNY sweater draped over that
chair, asking to be embraced, to be swept over
me, provoking my hair into a crazy frenzy
only to be swept into yet another organized
mess. The leaves bowed with attitude while I
dragged my boots across the slick cement,
swirling about my legs and stopping to rest on my messenger.

The scent of marijuana and Burberry hustled around
me like two people ready to settle an argument.
Vanilla, in its finest, tried to meditate the heat
only to be mistaken for this weak attempt.
I found it deep in my pocket.

> I kept playing the same track and hoped that it would
> bring me back. Couldn't stop my mind from teasing
> me with imagery of velvet and morning lust.
> It was over and, I was wandering to where I found comfort.
> Throwing my cigarette on the ground so it bounced into a
> puddle, I opened the door and said, "It's me, buzz me up."

My graduate supervisor once said: "If you get a PhD people will think you know what you're talking about; they'll listen to you." She was right, but she was wrong too. In academic settings you may need a doctorate degree in order to be taken seriously, but outside of that all you need is the truth. The truth doesn't require a doctorate degree. All it requires is itself—the simple, honest truth. It was simple, yet I've searched everywhere for the truth. The truth is quite difficult to find when those around you don't speak it or live in fear of it.

People listen to the truth. They may not like it, but when it comes, it is felt by the soul. I can make these statements with confidence simply because when I heard the truth it hit me deep in my heart. It was abrasive, yet gentle, and it stuck to my rib for days, months, weeks, even years after. It begged to be acknowledged.

The truth that so deeply hit my heart was that I was hopeless. This hopelessness that I held within was not something new. It grew out of my childhood and hadn't left my side since. I one day wondered why I always believed that I did not deserve love. I felt I did not deserve a good job, a well-behaved pet, nice shoes, a healthy body, or a comfortable home to live in. I could name a million menial and not-so-menial things, but you get the point. Even when something good happened to me, I always found myself waiting for it to suddenly go bad. I always waited for it to go south and turn to an utter disaster, and most of the time it did because I manifested and expected it to.

But sometime in my later twenties, the disaster part ceased. Positive things happened to me, but I still could not enjoy them for what they were. My cynical self always muttered under my breath, "This won't last, Jade. Don't get too comfortable with this joy thing, you'll be nothing but disappointed." Each statement closed my heart even tighter.

I was never told as a child, or even as an adolescent, that I could be anything I wanted, that I could get a good post-secondary education, that I could learn, write, and travel to different places. I was never encouraged or reassured that the world was my "oyster." I was never told that inside me was a place of such love and beauty.

It is very saddening to see a child, or anyone, filled with hopelessness. What you believe you are capable of, what you try, what you risk, what you never try, or say, or feel is based on the hopelessness you adopt as a child. I never asked to be hopeless. I don't think anyone does. I think that most of us, if not all, want to feel encouraged, free, and capable of doing anything. We all want to know that we are capable of feeling pure joy and that we have the energy to pursue our wildest dreams.

I've learned a very significant concept from understanding my hopelessness. That concept is that hopeless people cannot give hope. The only way to give hope is if you yourself feel hopeful. If those who I was surrounded by at a young age believed that they themselves were capable of anything they would surely have passed that beautiful ideology down to me.

Hopelessness affects us in every way imaginable. The more I thought about how hopelessness affected me, the more pissed

I became. How could my parents, the ones who were supposed to love me unconditionally, give me such a horrible gift of hopelessness? I was very angry and blamed them for this, as I was just a child. I viewed them as god-like, my protectors.

When I internalized what they taught me and started to behave accordingly, my parents disliked the results. The results were excessive drinking, negative emotions, judgment toward others, poor academic performance, and drug addiction. These results, I believe, were all influenced by the environment I was raised in. One could say I had a right to be angry, right? Yes, it is fair to say that the belief system I was taught in childhood caused me so much pain and harm, but it also allowed me to experience things that I know made amazing contributions to my wisdom bank and, in turn, this book. I have now come to forgive them and see these events as the building blocks of my story. They set the stage for my spiritual journey. This book aims to share the story of how someone who felt so unloved could find her way to love—not just any love, but God's love.

The overall theme of the chapter is that we as people cannot drink from an empty well. In other words, we cannot be filled by the emotionally unavailable, and we cannot be loved by the loveless. That sounds cynical and rather sad, but it is the truth. This notion helped with forgiveness, but I still felt angry and wanted to hold someone accountable. Why were they like that? The truth I have learned is that they are the way they are because of their own surroundings and experiences in their life (mostly childhood). Their parents trained them to be like them, and their parents' parents did the same. It is a cycle, and before long we are left with a repetitious pattern of emptiness and pain that is passed down from generation to generation. So the question becomes if I cannot get unconditional love from my parents and cannot blame them for not loving me and supporting me the way I most need and desire, who's responsibility is it to love me?

Mine!

It's no one else's job to love me. Not my parents, my boyfriend, spouse, the grocery store clerk, paperboy—no one. Sure, I'd like to think that it is indeed someone's role or obligation to love and care for me, but it's really not. It is my job, and if I looked in the right space I'd have seen it.

No, this isn't all there is. I don't feel loved and supported because I am around a bunch of people who fail to love and support themselves. And additionally, like I just mentioned and will reiterate another hundred times in this book, it is my job to love myself. We are the ones responsible for our own emotions, no one else.

This is where God came in.

I encountered the concept of God early on in my life. It was theoretical and slightly far-fetched. I used to think my grandmother was partially nuts. The way she talked about God was sweet, and I always thought to myself, "How cute, an old naïve woman talking about an omnipotent God who pays her bills and loves her more than any physical human being possibly could." She gave me books written by Max Lucado and I read them with curiosity. My father's mother also spoke of her love for God. Her accounts were brief but always filled with passion. A childhood family friend also cited Scripture to me and introduced me to a youth curricular program at a local church. I attended that program for a year, at least, with the other kids who lived on my block.

None of these three women—or anyone else I encountered then—ever really explained who God is with the truth and conviction I know now. None of them ever passionately showed me how powerful he is or, more importantly, what role I played in all of it. Who am I to God? Who is he to me? What does believing in God really mean? What changes in our minds or our lives when we begin to recognize and live by Jesus' teachings of love?

Before my change I always wondered why the intensity of love wasn't there. As I have just discussed, this was because all of these women still had roots in hopelessness, fear, and pain. They knew a concept of God, but not like I know God now. They knew of his love, but not like I do now.

The spiritual journey of coming to know God is highly personal. It is not one-size-fits-all. This later became a piece of wisdom that helped me in difficult times. Knowing that no two people share the same idea or experience of God helps me develop certainty and power in my own personal journey with God. For we can only know God through our experiences, and we all have a set of unique experiences here on Earth. This understanding led to a piece of wisdom. That is, we can only love something else (God, people, etc.) as much as we currently love ourselves. This is why my family and friends never spoke the love truth that pierced me. That was my answer. I need to love myself because I can't wait for others to fully love themselves in order to love me. I would die waiting! And sadly, most do.

I have control in this. I have a mission! That mission is to love myself and regain hope in my life. It is crucial that I state this again, for it is the main starting point for me in finding love: people can only love someone else as much as they currently love themselves. You cannot give what you do not have. Since God is love he can love me unconditionally. If he can love me, the next question is, can I?

CHAPTER 2

The Burning Question

Ask me again.
Ask me for assistance.
I'll take you to the valley where it all started, where
the dew embraced the green life that is I.
It will only hurt for a while. But in my promise I stand
by the notion that you will find abundance.
Ask me again.
Ask for my grace.
It will only last a night. When the new day dawns
you'll understand and the questions arise no more.

This chapter is about questions answered about loving oneself
and experiencing the joy and mystery that asking the right
questions at the right time brings. When all else is lost, there

must be that one curious flame still burning inside. It is hope, and it tells us that the story isn't over. It tells us that what we have experienced is never in vain but was experienced in order to bring divine knowledge. What we have experienced is never futile, and if we possess the courage to look beyond the surface we can see trauma, struggle, and hopelessness for what they really are: a really wild and unethical training camp. I believe that we all have the extra special opportunity to use our lives' circumstances for good, but it is up to us to dissect, to explore, and most importantly, to ask ourselves the right questions.

My journey started with asking the right questions. When I asked the right questions, God always brought the right people and events into my life to assist me in answering them. Sometimes the people engaged in the questions, other times people did something that brought out a feeling that led to answering the questions. The only thing that matters is that I came to a point where I started to ask the right questions. It's amazing how God orchestrates our lives; the people he brings in at exactly the right time. How it all works together. The more aware we become the easier we can witness the plan functioning like a well-oiled machine without attachment. Although I can't explain each and every occurrence in my life along with the specific purpose it has served, I am able to see the interconnectivity of my most significant life events.

My story is not glamorous. It carries sadness, but when I set out to actually produce a somewhat organized account of some of my experiences I knew that I had to be raw. I knew that I had to lay it out on the table. I do not know everything; I only know my story and how it changed me. I know that the greatest transformations for me were gained through truth. As a commitment to truth and because I am simply proud of the curriculum I have endured, I intend to share in the most candid way possible.

When asking the right questions, the next concept I learned was related to the first, which was you can only love someone as much as you love yourself. This new concept is just the opposite side of the coin, which is you can't hurt someone who is not already hurt inside. Many people disagree with this statement not because it is not true but because they want to blame others for their negative emotional states. The truth is that if someone says something that invokes a negative feeling within you, all they are doing is bringing to the surface what is already inside. Your emotional state is then put squarely in your hands. No one is responsible for your emotions but you. Jesus presented this concept when he said about those torturing him and killing him "Father forgive them for they do not know what they are doing" (Luke 23:34 NIV). He didn't say you are all going to hell for your actions, he asked God to forgive them.

If you remember what forgiveness is, it is love. Jesus was being killed and he still loved. How beautiful, and at the same time how scary! Can this be done? Can I hold myself accountable for all emotions that arise in me no matter what is done to me or said? The answer is yes, I can and I will.

CHAPTER 3

Don't Cry in My Cocaine

Let's run tonight.

Like every night, let's hide from the nagging suspicions.

Let's ignore the idea that I can do more than this.

Let's share our time with intoxication. Blur my lines, my morals.

Just blur my everything.

Just run and keeping looking back.

I used drugs for many years, pretty much any drug I could get my hands on. I wanted to be high. Always. My favorite of the many illicit drugs was cocaine. I used cocaine until my nose bled; until I was broke; until my mental state was so desolate and dark. I used cocaine in order to create a feeling, even if it was faulty, short-lived, and creating a huge detriment to my life. Cocaine makes it impossible to feel, impossible to be creative. For me, it stole my love for everything. I couldn't write, smile, or think of anything at all. I couldn't laugh with any degree of certainty or authenticity.

My peers made cocaine use seem acceptable. Even now when I hear people talk about their "wild years" they usually chalk it up to adolescence. They usually justify it with some half-valid excuse. But I wondered where that part of them went. I wondered that about myself.

The truth is that many people, when they quit an addiction, just switch to something more socially acceptable. They do not follow through to the root cause. They stop seeking when the addiction, the action, has stopped, and because they do not follow it through to the source they form a new socially acceptable addiction. They may not use cocaine anymore, but they may drink whiskey, gamble, workout, or whatever.

When you follow through to the source of an addiction, you find that the part deep inside that drove you to cocaine use did not really die. The action, yes, but the meaning behind using is still rampant in another form. If you take an onion, each layer is an addiction that grew from the center—hopelessness.

When I started out on my journey I believed that cocaine was my only problem, but as I went deeper and deeper into the meaning I learned that cocaine had many siblings. My story begins with my struggles to get over and heal from the pain of using cocaine.

I have many menacing memories related to using cocaine. The things I heard people say while on drugs and about drug abuse caused me great sadness and shame. The general energy that surrounds hardcore drug addiction is haunting. I don't care what anyone says, there is nothing happy about snorting cocaine until your hopelessness is dead, temporarily of course.

My drug addiction, like many other of my destructive behaviors, was brought on by the hopelessness I felt. My parents used alcohol on a regular basis, so undoubtedly as a child I learned that coping in that manner was okay or even good. I have tremendous compassion for anyone who is a slave to addiction, cocaine or otherwise. I later used my personal experience with cocaine addiction and recovery to pen a major paper for my master's degree, so in that way I can see that my experience with drugs served one of many significant purposes.

My boyfriend at the time and I used cocaine very heavily, often until four or five in the morning. When we ran out of cocaine or money we settled down to try to get some sleep. Anyone who is familiar with coming down off of a cocaine binge knows this is not a positive experience. We often had sex and smoked marijuana to try to ease the withdrawal symptoms.

I never felt as damaged, guilty, and worthless as I did in those early-morning moments. Our sexual experiences were so far away from love. I struggled with the memories of those early mornings for years. I often lied down, my nose red and pulsating with pain, and cried in silence. I seriously thought in those moments that dying would have been better than feeling what I felt. It was my lowest, and I hated every part of my life. I carried no purposefulness, and even though I knew that drug abuse was killing my spirit the only forward thought that would awaken a small sense of hope within me was that I would soon enough be high again.

Using cocaine couldn't happen often enough. When I wasn't high I was miserable. Angry and filled with regret, I often used violence and aggression to cope with my internal state. My relationship with my boyfriend was in a horrible state, and even though I knew that it couldn't possibly last I held onto misery with a grip so tight no one involved could breathe.

Cocaine served a very specific purpose for me. Rather than shame myself for years of abuse, I rejoice in the fact that without it I would have most likely committed suicide. Cocaine, in many ways, saved my life. It seemed counter-productive, but I am intelligent enough to know that it was the only option at that time. It was my crutch. I can see that God was in the cocaine. He knew I would see the other side of it, and even though my feelings about that were cynical, my spirit knew that it would eventually be used for good.

I relapsed a few times in the beginning stages of my recovery. This was hard because with relapsing came sadness. My ego used these experiences as a way of telling me that I hadn't changed and that I would struggle with this for the rest of my life. I had a clash of emotions because on one hand I was discouraged, and on the other I was proud that I had actually gone months without using. I believed that if I could function sober in the months in between that it was indeed feasible to quit altogether.

I've realized that with any addiction it is better to focus on the positive aspects of recovery. It is beneficial to be kind to ourselves, and even though it seems as if it will be a long, drawn-out struggle, if we focus on loving ourselves our addictions and their control over us will fade. I have found that love cures all destructive behavior and helps us focus on spiritual practices and relationship. You cannot rush the recovery process. I have found that each experience stayed in my life until it served its purpose and the lesson was learned.

Working through this addiction, I learned something new. I needed to be kind to myself. Hopelessness was the root cause of the true evil, and the more I became hopeful and started to release the guilt, the more love opened up within me. With many addictions there are usually more than one present. Cocaine was the worst by the standards of society, and it is what I focused on first. In my opinion, all addictions are the same. Whether it is illegal drugs, shopping, negative thoughts, praise, sex, going to church, it does not matter. All that matters is that deep down, addicted individuals do not love who they are and are searching for the answer to why externally. Once I started looking at my cocaine addiction and worked through it with love, I started to see another demon come to the surface. This one was older than the cocaine use and, as I found out, was part of the reason the cocaine abuse formed. My guilt over how I used my body was next on my radar.

We must use kindness when dealing with any of our addictions. We are not inherently bad people. We are not sinners no matter what drugs we've done or addictions we've struggled with. I have found that kindness toward the self goes a long way, and it can carry us through change with grace.

CHAPTER 4

My Body, My Life

He wants to know how far I'll go, how late I'll stay.
How many times will I kiss and retreat?
He wants to know how much I'll stray from my
agenda, leave my dignity on the floor.
How much can he destroy my sprit and how
much will I let him do just this?
How low can I bring you? Regret and regret.
Let me impose my childhood upon you. Let me
escape into you until you never feel again.
So like me, you never feel again.

Most people are afraid of telling others how many people they've been intimate with. How many people have you slept with? They justify withholding a response by saying some things we just must keep private. But we don't have to keep anything private. Only through secrets do we punish ourselves, harbor guilt, and carry things we don't need to. Through secrets we showcase our distrust for those we have the deepest relationships with. There is nothing wrong with that, because the truth is many people will react negatively to what you are hiding. But that is on them and speaks to where they are in their journey. It speaks to their character, never ours. Once you truly love yourself it does not matter what people say because all you see is God.

I have no shame at this point in my life, and I believe that the right people, the ones who read this without judgment, will find solace in my honesty. As I looked into this further I wanted to write a list of all the people I've had sexual encounters with in order to fully acknowledge the truth. This exercise taught me two things: it doesn't actually matter, and I have no clue. The list kept climbing and the shame started to rise. I don't remember who I've given the most personal parts of my body to. I don't remember who I've run from reality and true love with.

While looking at the list I realized God doesn't care how many people we've slept with. God only cares that we know how much he loves us and that we love ourselves. He only cares that we do not carry shame about our choices and experiences, sexual and otherwise. Louise Hay offers an amazing affirmation: "I love and approve of myself and I trust the process of life. I am safe" (Hay, 1999). I particularly like that one because it encompasses forgiveness, and to me forgiveness is the key to feeling unobstructed joy.

Many people would wonder why on earth I would be willing to tell anyone on God's green earth that I cannot name all my sexual partners. I am simply not concerned about sharing this because my inability to name or remember who I've given my body to is reflective of one very important thing, which is the meaning that drove that behavior. I also know that there are other people who indeed share this predicament, and although they intend to bring it to their final resting place, they carry it deep down inside every day. They may not have lists as extensive as mine, but I am sure that some may have at least a few sexual encounters they are not proud of. They may have only one person on their lists but may still carry the knowledge that the one person they gave their bodies to did not cherish, respect, or love them.

Knowing that you've been used—real or perceived—in that way can lead to some very deep negative feelings about yourself. But back to the reflection, my list of sexual partners is not extensive because I simply enjoy sex. It is because I have searched so desperately for someone to value me and love me. I have punished myself by finding and maintaining sexual relationships with broken people. I have willed sexual torment, abuse, and regret simply because of what I believed I deserved.

I truly believe with every part of my being that we create the situations that come into our lives. Our thought patterns, our deep-rooted belief systems attract our real life experiences. What is most saddening about what I am telling you is that my beliefs about what I was worth were so damaged that at one point I believed I was enjoying these relationships. Many of the men I've had sexual relationships with have treated me so poorly, knowingly or unknowingly, and the aftermath of those experiences has stayed with me for a large part of my life. Of course now that I have a better understanding of how I co-created those less-than-desirable circumstances I can move toward healing and forgiveness.

To help me see my sexual escapades as purposeful and reflective of my inner self-beliefs, God has shown me that he was right at my side during each and every moment. I often wonder why he allowed me to put myself out there in such a way, but soon after I realized it was part of the grand design. Just like the cocaine, God was in each sexual partner. Sex gave me false love, but that false love saved my life. Without that false love I probably would have committed suicide.

These experiences on our journeys, although sometimes they can be extreme and painful, have good fruit to come of them when viewed from a new perspective. I often turn to a favorite passage of mine that reads, "You intended to harm me, but God intended it for good to accomplish what is now being done, the saving of many lives" (Genesis 50:20 NIV). The ego tries to make you think that these experiences are bad, wrong, which builds up the guilt, shame, and regret. I now can say I see God in these experiences, and I approve of the choices I have made. I was not ready at that time to see what I see now. Because I see what I see now, I love myself and do not need to do what I used to do.

Some of my most painful memories come from various sexual experiences I've had. Some of the most intimate memories involving sexual encounters have created models of how I view sex even to this day. I, for some reason, have always thought that sex is a dirty act. I can honestly say that I've only had a true, loving sexual encounter with one person, and that was only after I learned to love myself. This is particularly sad to me because I have obviously been with more than one person.

I never knew why I was so open to giving myself to the less-than-deserving, but as I grew in spirit, faith, and love I learned a lot about my sexual past. It wasn't just that I was hopeless, but I've always tried to pay people with sex. I grew up feeling poor, and it was the only "currency" that I saw when I looked at myself. I couldn't offer love, joy, or happiness to anyone, so I offered sex. If I were wealthy I would have offered money to others for their fake love. When someone was nice to me and I couldn't return the favor with money or other material objects, I'd try to pay them with intimate sexual acts.

I was always a good, attentive lover, but there was always an element of emptiness in my intimate experiences. I've actually only encountered one person who showed me true love as he turned down my sexual advance. He said, "All you need to do is love yourself." I later learned that he was mindful of my pain and refused to allow me to further use sex to showcase my value. For someone so insecure who used sex as currency, this was both hurtful and shocking. As I stated before though, God brings people around to help you learn the answers you seek.

When it first happened I wondered how anyone could turn me down. What was wrong with me that he wasn't interested in my sex? It bothered me so deeply, and because of this rejection I went elsewhere. But once I became balanced again I saw God in that moment. I saw the old models and beliefs that came out. What God was saying was, "See how you seek acceptance through sex?" I understood that acceptance never really comes from those experiences because it can only come from inside. You give yourself to men, women, whoever, in pursuit of acceptance, but that is all it is—a pursuit. I wanted to have it every day.

Later I realized that his rejection of my sexual advances was one of the most genuine and profound acts of love I've ever experienced. He changed my ideas about men, sex, and self-worth. He was and still is a gift from God. This experience was the beginning of a sexual revolution of sorts. It marked the start of an amazing transformation in how I view sexuality. It was the beginning of a shift from guilt and shame to a positive perception of sex. Through this experience I was able to move toward opening my heart to the possibility that sex could be a spiritual experience, an act of sharing, joy, and pleasure.

CHAPTER 5

My Vision Is Not the Greatest

Look harder, look harder.
Look closer. Strain. But ask to see through his eyes.
Ask to see what he sees and he'll show you.
Ask to move past visions passed.
You squint and still it won't focus.
She must have said stop looking away, I cannot take your picture.
I won't want to let you, my beliefs are too crooked.
My beliefs are crooked like my eyes.
A dull pain that aches, they prescribe you
a solution and it never works.
Your glance is on inside, the looking glass begins with your heart.

I've worn glasses for the majority of my life. After a while we learn to accept our flaws. My poor vision has taught me many lessons. After countless conversations with God I realized that my need for corrective lenses is a metaphor. It is less about a physical ailment and more about a psychological one. I have conjured up many theories about why I have vision problems. I've read a number of metaphysical books; all of them offer possible explanations for poor vision. Most of them have to do with childhood socialization and how it may have impacted my ability to see clearly.

I think literature that offers metaphysical explanations for illness are amazing and serve a very distinctive purpose. But deeper than that, I believe that our illnesses and ailments allow us to discover how we truly feel about ourselves. I am very sure that my vision problems were created and maintained by a belief system. I identify as a person with poor vision and because of that, I am. Only when I truly believe with every part of my being that I am whole and healthy will I be just that.

I've had numerous experiences that have led me to believe that there is a distinct connection between our mental states and our physical wellness. I first understood this not by reading about it but by experiencing it. It was shocking, to say the least, but it opened my eyes to the connections of mind and body.

I had bladder infections for as long as I can remember before I started this new journey. I used to experience very painful bladder infections quite often, usually four per year, and I found that each time I had one I was caught in a cycle of negative thoughts about my promiscuous sexual behaviors.

I've heard people say that frequent sex leads to bladder infections for many women, it's quite common. That may be fair, but I carry a deep belief that mine were not because of my sexual actions but more related to the thoughts I had about those behaviors. Once I began to love myself, my bladder infections physically ceased even though my memory kept them alive. There have been many times since I started to place God and purpose in my sexual past that I have felt what I believed to be symptoms of a bladder infection, only to find out after seeing a physician that I did not have one. When I could finally look back and fully see God within my sexual encounters, I never had another bladder infection again. It has been over nine years now.

As I continued to work through some of the deep pain and sorrow, not only did my bladder infections go away but my skin got clearer, I had more energy, and I started to treat my body better. Even though I still engaged in sex (with the meaning being changed) my bladder infections never appeared again. I firmly believe that working through emotional and psychological suffering allows us to love ourselves more, and consequently our health and well being increases.

I would tell anyone who struggles with minor physical complications to work on increasing his or her love for him/ herself. Put God where you see pain. This is not to say that traditional medicine is wrong or unhelpful, because I believe God is in all the physicians who aid us in healing. But to incorporate love for who you are is, in my opinion, worth serious consideration.

As my feelings toward my sexual experiences changed positively, another addiction was shown to me. This one was deeper then the rest. This one started earlier than cocaine, and even earlier than sex. This linked to the other two in the form of acceptance and hopelessness, but was disguised by my weight and smoking.

CHAPTER 6

Still Hungry

This day my anxiety is palpable.
This day I'll criticize my form,
myself.
It makes me pass on the Bread of Life
and freedom.
I'll pass on everything.
If I could gain power and control of myself
I surely wouldn't starve tonight.

Women must cope with tremendous pressure when it comes to body image. It is no surprise to me that so many women I know struggle with weight, their appearance, and what they eat on a daily basis. I, like many people, was always told as a child that people wouldn't like me if I were overweight.

Counting calories now not only bores me to tears, it also actually scares me. I've figured out that counting calories or manically watching what we eat is a very futile attempt at control. If I have the power to rule over what I eat, I can effectively say that my life is under control. The message here is if you have to control every bite, every calorie, avoid certain foods and favor others, the fact of the matter is your life is probably already out of control.

I believe that the physical body is a tool for navigating through life. The variance in shapes and sizes is reflective of our uniqueness. The human body is amazing—what it can withstand, what it can do, what it can give. I am by no means an nutritional expert, nor do I know heaps about human anatomy, but I do know about love and its ability to create and maintain a healthy, functioning body and subsequently weight.

Jesus said, "Don't you see that whatever enters the mouth goes into the stomach and then out of the body? But the things that come out of the mouth come from the heart, and these make the man 'unclean'" (Matthew 15:17–18 NIV). I always interpreted this as it is not so important what we consume, but rather what comes out of our mouths. What we say is reflective of our love for ourselves. It is our love for ourselves that determines the true meaning of any eating.

I truly believe that it is less important to focus on what we eat and don't eat than it is to focus on creating a pure and open heart. I have found that through opening my heart my eating habits have changed for the better without extreme effort. I believe that when we focus on love our lifestyles start to reflect love. Not only does this impact how we as women feel about food, but it also impacts how we feel about everything. I believe it is of value to point out that dieting, although more socially accepted than overeating, is just another extreme rooted in hopelessness and fear.

Even though I was not doing cocaine and I was forgiving myself for the past sexual activities, I had an eating disorder. It didn't just pop up, it was linked to acceptance. Women not only strive to be a certain weight, they wax this and that, they wear make up or not, all in an effort to be accepted by the outside world. The eating disorder was just the answer I was looking for. It was God's answer to what I needed to focus on next.

The eating disorder really snuck up on me, and before I knew it I was 112 pounds of skin and bones. This may not be considered a low weight compared to others who struggle with eating and weight disorders, but for me it was scary and far too real. I was forced to acknowledge that I had a problem with food by the gift God had brought to me in the form of a comment a loved one made about my weight at Christmastime. I can only say that it came at the right time, and because of that I took notice and started to really look at what was going on in my life at that moment that made me want to gain control over my food intake.

At the time I was maintaining a few relationships that I knew were toxic and my inability to cut them off and move forward was killing me. Literally. When all this came into the light I found myself asking aloud, "At what point will I allow this to kill me?" I felt so alone with my disorder, ashamed, and afraid of whether I would ever get back to a healthy weight or not.

As a knee-jerk reaction I ate everything in sight in order to jumpstart my weight gain. This was pleasurable and exciting, and it felt great to just let go. I ate foods I had deprived myself of for two years prior. I heard my body yell, "Yes! Yes! Go!

Go!" I learned something very important about weight and eating during that experience. Most importantly, God's love for us is not dictated by our weight or what clothes we fit into or don't. God's love penetrates deep beyond our ideas of beauty or ideal body types. God's deepest desire for us is that we love ourselves, and through that love we are able to love another without condition.

When we love and accept ourselves we automatically become the weight we are supposed to be. When we love ourselves and the world around us we automatically exercise enough to create a healthy lifestyle. I have found that there is no effort needed no maintenance required. I now follow my intuition, and because I've spent so much time getting to know God, he encourages me to eat vanilla cake when the mood strikes me and eat spinach salad for dinner when that feels right.

One of the most valuable things I've learned is that we should always feel comfortable. Wherever there is anxiety and stress, God is not. Wherever there is worry, regret, and sadness, God is not. Everything that is God is love. Everything that is God feels good, joyful, and grateful. When we are connected to God and his perfect love we will feel at ease. Everything that is complicated and anxiety provoking is far away from God. Straining and working hard at getting thin is not comfortable or, in my experience, fun. I now tend to base where my heart is in relation to God on how much anxiety, worry, or stress I am carrying.

Dieting and counting calories is, in my opinion, no more positive than eating ourselves into poor states of physical and mental health. They are the same. They are both reflective of unstable emotions and pain. I came to this conclusion after I realized that one of my friends, who was quite overweight, seemed to be overeating for the same or similar reasons as I was starving myself. At one point I thought that I was the good and responsible one, but the fact is that we both just used different actions to express the same feelings of deep-rooted hopelessness, need for acceptance, and desire for control. This observation brought me to the notion that while on a spiritual journey it is crucial to look at the meaning behind the action itself. It has brought me understanding to realize that meaning is *everything*. Jesus describes this concept in many ways, one of which is when he states in Matthew 6:1, "Be careful not to do your acts of righteousness in front of men, to be seen by them," and again when he says in Matthew 6:16, "When you fast do not look somber as the hypocrites do, for they disfigure their faces to show men they are fasting. I tell you the truth, they have received their reward in full. But when you fast put oil on your head and wash your face, so that it will not be obvious to men that you are fasting, but only to your Father, who is unseen; and your Father, who sees what is done in secret, will reward you." It would be impossible for me to open my heart without knowing deep in my being that I cannot judge by action alone. I could not gain understanding without exploring the meaning behind action.

After I seriously acknowledged the feelings I had about myself, my childhood, my emotional pain, the weight struggle went away. One day I got out of the shower and looked at myself in the mirror. I started to weep, tears streamed down my face and I just stood there for the greater part of half an hour amazed by my beauty. That might sound a little foolish to some, but for someone like me who felt disgusted when I looked in the mirror for years, it was an accomplishment. It was pure satisfaction. In that moment time stood still and I saw myself the way God saw me. It was nothing short of magical.

This was the first time in my life that I could even consider seeing myself as God saw me—perfect. My body was so beautiful that I likened myself to an angel. I knew that I was in a very good space when I couldn't find a single thing I would change.

I used to compare myself to other women, always looking for something to compare and criticize. Now when I'm in public I see radiant beauty in other women, but I never feel less than. I never feel as though I am missing something or long for something they have and I don't. I sometimes feel slight sadness, as most of the women I encounter are still punishing themselves for their perceived lack of beauty in some significant way. They all have looks of lament and exhaustion. They need to know what I do. Stop working at the wrong aspects of yourself. There is only one answer to all your weight problems, and it is love.

CHAPTER 7

Do It Like This

Do it like me. Ask no questions, but place your life in my ways.
I'll show you how to live even if you pay later.
Watch my actions and live those. Breathe those. Tell
everyone that I am God. Treat me as such.
When this fails no one will be held responsible.
Do it like this.
Even if it feels bad.
Even if you lie to yourself, live like me.
I know the way.
Live. Like. Me.

We try to gain acceptance from our parents in many ways. I was unconscious of the ways I tried to gain acceptance from my parents. I didn't realize until much later that I felt that if I mirrored my parents' behaviors I would gain more respect and love from them.

As a young child I saw both my parents smoke. I used to steal cigarettes from my mother in the fifth grade. I would take a pack from her drawer in the morning before school and at lunchtime my friends and I would smoke them. I don't know if my mother knew I was stealing her cigarettes or not, but I don't remember her ever scolding me for it.

I was in my late twenties when I first tried to quit smoking. I thought I was driven to quit for health reasons and because of the stigma attached to it. My first attempt failed and I knew the reason for the "failure" was because I wasn't focused on the reason I started. If we fail to consider the true reason we start and maintain a smoking habit all attempts at quitting will be unsuccessful. Or, as mentioned before, the addiction will just change to something else. I realized that my smoking was not directly related to the tobacco addiction itself, but rather to a connection I made between smoking and my parents when I was much younger. I believe we often justify our behaviors—addictions included—without ever considering where and when they first started. Why does anyone just pick up smoking? Why do we continue into our adult years?

I assumed I was addicted to smoking like I was once addicted to using cocaine, but after serious reflection I noticed that my smoking behaviors had more driving them then what was on the surface. I would recommend focusing on your individual reason for starting smoking or any other addictive behavior and question the events that preceded the initial smoking experience. Look at the person(s) who gave you your first cigarette or told you that it was appropriate behavior. Once we reflect on these circumstances we can begin to gain insight into the strength and nature of our relationship to the substance, in this case, smoking.

We can never move past an addiction before it has finished its course. It is crucial to learn to love ourselves first and lessen our focus on the action itself. I truly believe that when we do the work, the negative or undesired action will fall away effortlessly. We do not have to focus on quitting smoking, but rather redirect our attention to why we chose to deprive ourselves of freedom and in turn, a healthy lifestyle.

One of the most significant lessons I've learned in my spiritual journey is that anything that comes from love, from God, will never make me feel bad. If my connection with God is alive, and indeed it is, I should never feel as if I am not doing enough. Guilt and God do not belong in the same sentence, paragraph, or encyclopedia. I can do no wrong. Nothing I have done should make me feel guilty. I should never harbor the belief that I am not doing enough or that I should be doing this, that, or the other thing.

The spiritual journey runs its own process. God's timing and being kind toward yourself yields good fruit. I have found that focusing on getting rid of bad behaviors is counter-productive. I have made several attempts to speed up the process, which was really evident with smoking. I would throw away a full pack of cigarettes only to find myself smoking as early as three days later.

It is important that we focus on love. In due time the behaviors that aren't healthy for you will vanish effortlessly. And by that time, you won't care either way. The attachments and aversions will be dead. Each attachment mentioned throughout this book has gone. I have gone back to a couple, as I mentioned with sex and sometimes smoking, but the meaning is completely different.

CHAPTER 8

Quiet My Mind,
It Works Too Hard

Come to me.
Drink my water.
You'll never go thirsty. You'll banish thoughts that bind
your life. Your salvation is waiting, if you so desire it.
The greatest freedom is a free mind. A free mind never
starts in the past or focuses on the next quarter.
It is now.

My greatest struggle in the past eight years has not been releasing physical addictions—whether cocaine, sex use, or image issues—it has been working with my mind. There is nothing more truly scary for the mind, the ego, than a statement that says I love myself.

Because of this journey toward love, I've really gotten to know my mind. My mind has been extremely overworked and undercompensated throughout my life. I could not get my mind to stop or a single minute. I've struggled with extreme anxiety throughout this journey. I spent hours caressing every single negative thought I had. Many of those thoughts were punishing thoughts, my favorites being *I'm a failure, no one loves me, I am terminally ill,* and *I am only worthy of abandonment.*

I had severe health anxieties. I've had every illness you can imagine, though solely in my mind, of course. I would spend the majority of my day checking my skin, teeth, and every other part of my body for abnormalities. They rarely materialized, but if I gave them enough fuel they would meet my demands and manifest as a weird rash or pain. This was another experience that contributed to the idea that there was indeed a connection between my mind and body.

I had read some articles about the mind–body relationship by now, but no scholarly article validated this idea like my personal experience. I would often lie in bed at night and silently worry myself to sleep. I shared the intensity of my thoughts with few people. My anxiety issues were great, and as I became more inquisitive and familiar with my mental processes, I realized that I required a power greater than human intellect to truly set me free of my suffering.

I needed something that went beyond the idea of good and bad thoughts. Although I knew God and had developed a meaningful relationship with him, I wasn't feeling the security and peace that I knew only his love could provide. I knew I needed to drink further in the Spirit. I needed the assurance and peace that come with knowing that God is inside me, and if I could maintain that one-pointedness I could feel joy and move out of the realm of fear and constant doubt.

I cannot say that I have moved beyond my thoughts completely, but they no longer carry the power they once had. I am so extremely mindful of my thoughts that now when I have a thought I can witness it, call it out, feel it, and release it. I often use affirmations such as, "I am not my negative thoughts," and, "This thought is simply a reaction to the pure loving awareness that is coming into my life at this time." I find that if I don't give my thoughts any food they quickly leave with haste. Of course they return to try to conquer my joy again, but the duration and frequency have lessened significantly.

I've learned that no negative thought we have about ourselves or our lives ever comes from love. Complicated and threatening thoughts come from a dark place, as I mentioned before. They come only from my past, lies I believed before. Negative thoughts come out of judgment, guilt, shame, and hopelessness. God is none of those things, nor does he stand for any of that. Everything that comes from God's pure love is rooted in kindness. They are compassionate. I've changed my life quite significantly through nursing positive thoughts. I used to believe that negative thought processes would always win, but that's never true. Love is more powerful, and it changes us from the inside out.

I now understand that this worrying mind was created before all the other addictions I have discussed. The worrying mind was one of the first addictions that was created in me since I was just a baby. This worrying mind was the catalyst in forming the beginnings of helplessness and fear. Hence, it was the last of the four areas I had to conquer with love.

I could understand how all of the other addictions benefited me in my survival, but how can worrying be seen as good? I always dealt with the past, but this challenged me in a new way. It made me face the future. When we worry, it is always about the future. The future can be scary, but after I loved myself I needed to love God. I needed to develop the faith to say God has the future under control, what he brings to me, I will see with love.

This idea that worry can actually be the catalyst to the development of faith was what I needed to understand the beauty in my worrying mind. Thank you, Lord, for giving me the wisdom to see the beauty in the suffering. I am where I am because of this worrying mind, and I love it! I love who I have become!

The wisdom that I gained through this experience was learning to quiet my mind, to be in the present, not the past or future. Possess a faith like the Roman soldier's (Matthew 8:10), know God has the future in his perfect hands. There are different ways to quiet your mind, a couple of them are found in mediation and prayer. This is the method I have used and it has been most helpful in remaining in the present. Just as with learning anything new, it took time and effort. But with true determination and kindness toward myself, God opened my mind to the moment. I have found that there is nothing more profound and beautiful than the current moment, our calmed breath reminding us that we are indeed alive and well.

CHAPTER 9

Ram Dass, My Heart Sings for You

Queen of the universe, you sleep late and he loves you deeply.
The water cleanses if you let it, open your heart.
He is there, in your cup
watching you hold back tears, and just force
this smile another afternoon.
You punish and he wonders why
You don't need to, need to stay late,
work hard and clean.
No expectations for the queen.
You earn the crown without merit.
Queen of the universe, she stays the most beautiful of all.
They all stay the most beautiful of all

What am I? If I'm not who they said I was or even who I thought I was, then who could I be? And who is everyone else? The problem with using society as a mirror is the fact that they can only view you the way they see themselves. Not who they say they see when they look into the mirror, but how they truly see themselves. I wasn't often told that I was a junkie or a useless drug addict since most of my friends had similar addictions. However some people who had different addictions ventured out to make their sentiments known to me and treated me like a parasite.

My social interactions with other users were riddled with cynicism and deceit. That was just the way I liked it, and for many years it kept the lie alive. They feed my delusion and I would do the same in return. This happens outside the world of drug abusers as well. Of course, I didn't see the saturation of this until my thinking mind uncovered the intensity much later.

A beloved spiritual teacher of mine, Ram Dass once said in one of his lectures that we spend most of our lives asking and affirming that our masks are on straight, alluding, of course, to the identity masks we wear. The blatant problem with this is that our perceived masks are not our real masks, and my thinking mind uncovered that in time as well. Our perceived masks convince us that we are weak, inadequate, and powerless. Our perceived masks are either riddled with false confidence or utter despair. I happened to like both. I happened to pretend I was confident, yet on the inside I never felt like I was.

Neither of these stances are so important now because there are obvious shortcomings associated with both exuding false confidence and feeling completely useless on the inside. The most notable shortcoming is that both stances lack the element of just being love. In order to just be love one isn't required to do anything. When you are in a state of love, there is no doing. It all just flows out like a river to a lake. You witness each act inside and are filled with joy.

I was once completely controlled by things I didn't even know existed. These elements were major contributors to the shaping of my perceived identity. The irony of the zombie craze right now is that the larger part of society are characterized as zombie-like and don't even have a conscious awareness of it. The idea that we are independent freethinkers is a lie, for until you work through past beliefs about the world and yourself you just relive those beliefs over and over whenever you make choices. You are never fully able to choose based on the moment, not the past or the future, but the love of the moment.

I've spent most of my life thinking I'm something I'm not. I was always a different person depending on who was around. I often said yes to others and in turn, no to myself. This brought deep feelings of sadness and dissonance. I always considered myself to be real and I really wasn't. I've done many things that I thought would please my parents, my boyfriends, and friends even though they often made me uncomfortable. I was so afraid to tell or show people who I was becoming, afraid of being inconsistent in my journey. My choices were often erratic and I've struggled to find my way to peace and self-acceptance. I always had this feeling that if I didn't comply with the general population's idea of likeable I would be rejected, and ultimately I was.

When I began to realize that I was surrounding myself with very sad, cynical individuals who constantly viewed themselves as victims, I noticed the impact it was having on my life. When you change, the truth is it can be lonely. The people in your life—whether friends or family—begin to look much different to you. God may bring them closer to you, but usually, as I have found, there is separation because your attachments weaken.

Though it was lonely as old friends faded, God always brought new people around me to share in the love of this moment and my spiritual journey. I don't want to convey the idea that everyone I was surrounded by was all doom and gloom. Most of them weren't conscious of it and still aren't. Some of the people who have come into my life over the last several years considered themselves God-loving individuals, and I have no doubt that they believed they were. I also have no doubt that they had some type of relationship with God, but something seemed off about them. They didn't seem happy or even content. I often heard them say things that I felt were misinterpretations of God's Word, things like smoking will take you to straight to hell. To me, hell denotes punishment, and the God I know never offers conditional love.

The Holy Bible says something along the lines of "seek and you will find; knock at the door and the truth, God, will be revealed to you." This is so true. Most people do not meet God in His purest form not because He is not there but because they don't really want to. God is always right behind the partition we've created. This is shown in the statement by Paramahansa Yogananda, "You do not have to struggle to reach God, but you do have to struggle to tear away the self-created veil that hides him from you."

I didn't encounter God in all his glory until I came to a place where I was absolutely desperate for him. I prayed and thanked him day in and day out, and I believed in my heart that he would reveal himself to me when the time was perfect.

Most people I've encountered aren't willing to give anything up to meet him. Our attachments, known or unknown, keep us from taking a risk and letting go of what has given us comfort. Even if those things have made us unhappy. Most people I've encountered want to maintain the comforts of ego stroking, of routine conformity, of what they consider to be normalcy. They want him in their darkest moments, but when they begin to feel better they realize they are just fine on their own without him. I've found that most people ask for God half-heartedly. They ask for Him with a slight of mind or a half-convincing shout, as a temporary assistance type of request. Most people don't ask for God with everything.

But when you are tired of suffering and the constant dance of insecurity, tired of trying to lose weight and failing, pouring another drink when you actually don't want to, when you can no longer stand mindless gossip, you begin look for something else. You look for light and love and all that is God. Your body aches for peace and just one moment that you can look into the mirror and feel joy or feel acceptance toward your life, your choices.

When you want to look in the mirror and feel proud of the way you spend every minute of your life, you'll seek him. As I mentioned previously, I refer to God because he is my definition of unconditional love. Some people get to the place I'm talking about and just beg for change and love without ever saying God, or calling the name of Jesus. I'm not so concerned with what you call him and I don't believe he is either, but I believe that God and love are interchangeable terms. The moral of this chapter is simply when you no longer want to hide your thoughts from your family, and more importantly yourself, you'll look for him, for unconditional love, with relentless desire and intensity.

God has revealed himself to me through the most amazing and wondrous forms. Some of my greatest teachers I don't know on a personal level, but they reveal they are doing God's work. They may not label themselves as devotees of Christ in particular, but they identified that they indeed are in the business of spreading love and positivity.

A few years into my spiritual journey I felt very isolated and alone. My desires had changed quickly, and I had experiences that I couldn't share or even put into words if I tried. I only had one other person, who I am tremendously grateful for, with whom I could discuss my obscure spiritual experiences. Beyond that, my connection with my closest friends diminished and soon I found myself not wanting to spend time doing what they were doing. I didn't share the same values anymore, and the idea of sitting around in constant complaint made me extremely hopeless, anxious, and exhausted.

There were many nights when I asked God and myself if I was going crazy. How could I be changing so quickly? How could things I cared so deeply for just one year ago be so far away from me? This wasn't a change in latté or nail polish color preference, this was a deep inner transformation. How I felt about friends, family, major social problems, suffering, romantic relationships, and money was all changing, and not just a little. It was dramatic, and it was as if it was going to keep changing regardless of how I felt about it. It was as if I was on a rollercoaster and I was completely unable to get off.

I, however, didn't want to get off. As much as I felt isolated, I knew in my heart that this road would lead to joy and happiness. Not so much the type of happiness I saw in Hollywood movies, but pure and utter joy. I was committed to moving forward, and at that time of loneliness I still felt a sense of trust that all this change was working for good. I felt that a gift was awaiting me, and when I got to the place where I could open it I wouldn't regret letting go of what I once believed to be the truth.

I somehow came across an audio file on iTunes. I often searched out different lectures or recorded talks that provided deeper understanding regarding my walk with God. Not religious materials, but material about a mutual spiritual relationship. I searched for someone or something that could align or explain what I was going through. I found many people who prompted me to further understand the teachings of Jesus, but something felt off. It felt incomplete.

Many books or lectures I listened to or read seemed to be missing something. Many of them carried a slight hint of threat, judgment, and worst of all, conditional love: do this for God's love. It seemed to me that God's love was placed into a small, well-defined box, and this did not align with my experience. I knew God, even this early in my journey, to be grand, to be limitless, and to never impose conditions on anything.

The audio file I discovered was titled *Finding and Exploring Your Spiritual Path*. It was a rather dated recording of a man named Ram Dass, a former Harvard professor. I listened to the tape the first night on my iPod, on my bed, in complete darkness. As he started to talk my heart opened and became full. I connected with him because he was a scholar and I was an undergraduate student at the time. Greater than the academic connection was a spiritual one. He detailed every single feeling and experience I'd had over the three years prior to listening to this recording. I remember feeling so filled with joy. In that moment I felt two very important things: solidarity and I wasn't crazy. It was a gift from God. It validated me. It helped with the shame of my heavy drug use. I often thought to myself, "If Ram Dass could do LSD and be this loving, I can surely move past the shame of this cocaine addiction." It took my relationship with God to a whole new level. I listened to that recording until my iPod burnt right out and would no longer function.

Ram Dass had such an eloquent, witty, and fun-loving way of illustrating his experiences with academia, his family relations, and most importantly, the love his guru showed him. I longed to encounter Ram Dass, and although I have spent these several years building the most amazing connection with him my heart longs to one day express my gratitude to him.

In many ways, Ram Dass saved my life. As his name means, he truly was a servant of God. I knew that God was surely aware of the impact his lectures would have on my life, and in countless situations I used his reflection of unconditional love to cope with daily stress. I bought every single audio recording I could find, and the more I listened and memorized and the more confident and loved I felt. When my birthday came I asked anyone and everyone for iTunes gift cards because I was struggling financially and knew that Ram Dass could feed me like nothing else could.

As I moved forward with my journey I began to look for other birds of the same feather. I wondered who else was out there whom I could learn from. My goal, as mentioned in the introduction of this book, was to quiet my mind and open my heart, so I was on the prowl for wisdom, and I was open to anything and everything.

These people rarely, if ever, know that I see them as God and would most likely label me as nuts if they knew I saw them as such. The most profound teachers have been spiritual teachers who I feel a deep connection with, whom I have encountered in both my dreams and waking life. God used many people to show me many different things, but once I requested to know God on a deeper level he began to lead me to different spiritual teachers. These teachers, with their unique experiences and unique ways of articulating their experiences, each taught me valuable lessons about getting closer to God.

Eckhart Tolle, through his lectures, taught me to quiet my mind and focus on unity. His lighthearted laugh brings me much joy, and I revel at his simplicity and compassion. As for Ram Dass, I reveled in his amazing wit and experiences with psychedelics and guru Maharaji. Wayne Dyer emphasizes the power of the human mind, positive thought, and our magnificent ability to co-create. Paramahansa Yogananda, teaches what is truly possible with God.

The way God uses different people to further our growth is amazing. I am captivated by the way that our wonderful God instills hope in humanity through people. My loving connection with these individuals has fostered a deep sense of awareness of the above-mentioned, and I am grateful that their teachings have been available to me.

The point to be made here is simply that once we set out to learn, grow, and open our hearts, God begins to put the plan in motion. Only when we agree to open our hearts and allow God to change and mold us can he lead us to salvation, redemption, and love. The greatest thing we can do is be flexible. A closed mind is a fearful mind, and a fearful mind refuses to fully consider love.

CHAPTER 10

It's All Perfect

I'll cry tonight, I'll say I don't feel you like I should.
We are alone with our thoughts and divine nothingness.
You got me to read the passage and I
could barely mutter the words.
My sobbing took over and then you encouraged me to yell them.
Get them out, feel my power. Here and now, feel my grand power.
Hold me, because tonight I'll cry.
Tonight I'll cry, but not for the same reason.
I'll cry with joy, amazement of your ways.
The psalms made promises, and you see them through to the end.
Tonight I'll cry at your methods.
I'll cry because you care and love more than I understand.
I'll cry with relief because it's all perfect.
My tears say with exhaustion:
I'm catching on.

I used to believe in mistakes. I used to believe in shame and often thought that if I could go back and fix things I would. It's taken me years to get to a place where I see functionality in everything. Before I gave up on a psychological perspective of everything I relied on it heavily. After hours and hours of deep reflection and thought I understood that because of my general feelings of inadequacy I resorted to harmful behaviors. I thought that because I never felt truly loved I sought out the love of others, most notably men. All of that may hold some truth, but at this point I'm not so much concerned with blaming others for my hardship.

God is beyond psychology. Beyond the psychological level there is a greater power and the need to understand everything diminishes. God is an engineer who develops the neuroses necessary to provide us with what we need to learn. My suffering—psychological, emotional, and physical—has always been part of a bigger plan. Far before I knew God, he was working in my life. I don't know exactly why I have had to experience exactly what I have, but I do know it serves a greater purpose. I often feel as if I know why I have gone through what I have when I connect with others. Dealing with addictions especially has allowed me to develop a deep compassion for others who have struggled with the same adversity.

Suffering has burned through me in many ways, and as I look at my past I can clearly see that my suffering was what so delicately brought me close to God. It has brought me great humility. I am grateful and in awe of the power of God, and I have learned that God's ways are certainly not my own. His methods, although at times have seemed absolutely crazy, were very necessary.

God never does a single thing without a divine purpose, and it all works for good. No matter how I saw it at the time, I am confident that it all is perfect. Many people who have endured suffering get upset when I make such statements, but I know that perception is everything and how we use and evolve from our suffering is our choice. At any point I could have identified with my suffering too deeply and allowed it to consume me. Trusting in God has allowed me to pull hope from even the most hopeless situations. In many ways the negative situations or relationships I've endured were reflective of my own wanting. When I believed that I deserved shallow relationships that was exactly what I attracted into my life. I often got into habits of finding people who would behave in accordance with how I felt about myself.

God has given me every experience I've had with purpose. If I could go back and alter my past I wouldn't. To carry a desire to change my past comes with the assumption that God has messed up. God simply does not mess up—*ever.*

My life has been filled with amazing miracles. I've come from places so dark into God's perfect light, and for that I am beyond grateful. Understanding that God has been right beside me through my entire journey has given me great pleasure, and I find the most comfort in knowing this. Nothing I have endured has been in vain, and I am astonished at the grandeur of God's wonder-working plan. In my eyes there is nothing comparable to the impeccable timing of God and his intervention. I am right where I need to be at this point in my life, and I find that accepting this reduces both guilt and pressure tremendously.

When we rely on God and his perfect love our need for control diminishes and suddenly we experience the joy that comes with trusting a higher power. My greatest shifts have been both initiated and processed by doing absolutely nothing, just being love. When I am still and inquisitive, but not too inquisitive, I learn the most about myself.

CHAPTER 11

Vulnerable for Life (The Termination)

Out by the garden. Tend to it and love it.
Tend to it and release the nutrients.
The colors and wishing.
The paints of the wheel, they sit in harmony. Out by
the garden we grow and feed off one another.
Show me how to thrive and I'll protect your heart.
Show me how to live and thrive. Catch my tears out
by the garden and return to me with lush love.
Out by the garden we reach to the sun.
We reach for the purest love. You laugh and
all the trails of life are on your face.
No fears because love cannot flourish this way.
Take a breath and thrive.

> Today, overcast and threatening, we fear not. Out
> in the garden the rain is welcomed and it always
> greets our souls with promise of change.

I've spent some time doing research on addiction. My personal experience with addiction says I'm an expert, but my scholarly achievements say I'm not. I'm not concerned with how anyone reading this wants to classify me in order to feel comfortable. That's your business.

I've read a considerable number of books and articles on addiction and recovery, all written from different perspectives. They are all amazing. I'm not just saying that because I feel a need to needlessly congratulate every single person who has ever done research on addiction and recovery, but because I believe that they each have something significant to offer. There are many perspectives of addiction, and they obviously vary by discipline. There is research from the viewpoint of clinicians, sociologists, criminologists, and of course the less recognized sources, addicts or former addicts themselves.

Most people I talk to about addiction or alcoholism say things like, "One drink can kill a recovering alcoholic." "Addicts are in recovery for life!" "They will always have to walk on eggshells." I dislike these types of statements for two reasons. First, way to be optimistic! Nothing says fear and weakness like statements such as those. I don't assume that about people. I'd like to assume that there comes a point in one's life when he or she is no longer on guard. If you truly uncover and deal with why you abused drugs, alcohol, sex, etc., in the first place you won't be vulnerable for life.

Oftentimes people in recovery are destined to identify as people in recovery for the remainder of their lives, and that is obviously trapping for so many reasons. There was a time when I was so vulnerable that I couldn't even watch *Scarface* or *Blow* without going into a state of major panic. There was a time when I feared that someone I was around would unexpectedly pull out a tiny plastic bag of cocaine and offer me a line. How would I respond to that? I only felt insecure about such situations because I wasn't fully over my addiction. There were parts of myself that did not understand the grand design, my power, my God.

When I meet people they often say to me, "Your addiction seems so far from you. At this time in my life, yes, my cocaine addiction is far from me. I do not struggle every day to maintain sobriety. I do not have days where I want to score a gram of cocaine and start using again. Many current cocaine addicts would be happy to hear that you can definitely get to a point where you don't even think of using. You can get to a point where you don't feel it necessary to judge and criticize people who are still using in order to feel strong in your recovery. In no way am I saying that there isn't a phase of vulnerability and healing, but the idea that we will be vulnerable for life is, in my opinion, false. If you conquer your addiction with the right tools and seriously engage in learning self-love and acceptance you can kill your addiction and eliminate the probability of it shape-shifting into another.

The Bible says, "Therefore, if anyone is in Christ, he is a new creation; the old has gone, the new has come!" (2 Corinthians 5:17 NIV). It is difficult to move past an old identity. Many of us identify with social roles so deeply that it causes us to suffer. As my spiritual journey progressed I noticed how social roles, although they serve a distinct purpose, limit our lives. When we identify as young, beautiful, mother, student we automatically expect those in our lives to see us as that.

We all play countless roles on any given day, but attachment to those roles can be a detriment to our growth. Seeing myself as an addict or recovering addict—among several other negative labels such as criminal, whore, damaged, and useless—caused me to behave in ways that were not even true to my being. In other words, even after I had significantly changed, I was holding on to old models of myself, and that made me to want to act out these labels. The problem with labels, given to us by our own account or by others, is that we tend to internalize them.

I knew I had done some major work when I had a dream in which I walked past a table with a mountain of cocaine on it and felt absolutely nothing—no deprivation, no angst, no regret. That may sound strange to anyone else, but I connect to my dreams and how they reflect my spiritual progress. My dreams have been amazing indicators of my spiritual wellbeing and have even been pre-cognitive in nature on occasion. I find the more I give credit to my dreams for helping me, the more they step up to the plate in awkward times of growth.

The point that I aim to make here is that I don't believe that formerly addicted people will always be vulnerable. I don't believe that we are forced to always be alert to our past. We can let it go. We can heal, learn, and destroy our attachment to substances and the pain and suffering that maintained our addictions. I believe that we can get to a neutral space where we no longer view our drug of choice as the Devil.

Now, I don't feel any positive or loving feelings toward cocaine per se, but at the same time I don't feel afraid of it. I don't feel threatened by it. I see the role it played in my life. I see how it helped me cope. At this point in my recovery I don't feel controlled by cocaine use or the lack of it. I can confidently say that my feelings toward it are neutral. In a way I feel as though I have forgiven cocaine and it's done the same for me.

I believe that every single person who struggles with substance abuse can arrive at a place where they no longer feel substances have an undying hold on their bodies and consciousness. I also believe that this is one of the greatest accomplishments an individual can experience.

CHAPTER 12

Love Lives Here

We are supported, and my white linen
dress matches the inside of me.
It ruffles around my leg gently in the wind.
I am a human angel, so delicate and precious.
I see beauty in everything, and where I hid
from bees I now go with rigor.
They speak softly, showing me their purpose.
They all share their purpose,
speaking softly when sharing.
The angels always appreciate a calmed assured voice.

To acknowledge someone else's suffering is quite difficult. In order to do so, you have to see your own. The same goes for beauty and worth. To see it within you is to see it in others.

Someone who sees only negative aspects of their life will walk around seeing just that in everything else.

One of the million things I like about God is that he can carry all the burdens you place upon him. He will always listen to your rants about feeling invalidated, unimportant and after you've detailed these he whispers, "My love will compensate all other shortcomings. My love will come to you easily and you'll never have to ask me to care for you."

Caring is God's business. I have come to realize that everything that my parents, friends, or boyfriends were not, God was. His love outshined everyone because he was love. I didn't have to be skinny, smoke, or offer sex to be accepted. He accepted me, and more than that, he loved me so much that he could change my entire life from negative to positive when I just opened my heart and quieted my mind.

Surrendering myself to God has activated some changes, all of them amazing! Through trusting him I have learned to love, forgive, and repent. Nothing has humbled me more than my relationship with God. He gives and takes away, and the moment you decide that you will let go of your attachments for a greater good, he begins to work in new ways. With me he began to work quickly. I always felt so good when I was praising him. I have struggled with how others would perceive me. How can a girl who lived such a reckless lifestyle be a Christian?

I don't exactly adore the word *Christian* simply because I feel it places people in a box that they cannot uphold. To me, loving God is just that. If other people feel comfort in calling me a Christian it's fine by me. Jesus is the door that I enter to feel and experience unconditional love. I believe in Jesus. I believe in his power and his existence. At the same time, I am open to believing in who others claim their God to be as well. As long as the source is pure loving awareness I am in on it.

People get rather upset about denominations and the point is often missed. My main is concerns are love, kindness, and forgiveness. With that being said, I happen to personally fancy Jesus because of our personal connection. Jesus is a reflection of unconditional love and to me, a gateway to perfect peace.

I wish to close this book with a letter I wrote to myself. I referred to this letter while writing this book whenever I felt doubt about actually sending a piece of my life out into the world for everyone to see. I will tell you that I now have more joy-filled days than bad. I feel happiness more than sorrow, and my life has opened up like a blossoming flower. I know that whatever humanity struggles with can be healed through love.

I believe violence, addiction, and abuse, self-inflicted or otherwise, all carry a very strong presence and energy. Negative emotions can linger for years, and getting over the most hurtful experiences of our lives is surely not an easy task. But more than that, I know that nothing carries more energy or power than love. Love can abolish all pain and conquer even the most desolate and dark situations. There is always hope if we agree and commit to living with quiet minds and open, loving hearts.

Dearest Jade,

I am writing this letter to remind and inspire you. I am so proud of you for sharing your story with the world. Please know that by putting your story out into the universe you have indeed glorified God. I know you have had doubts about allowing such personal and sometimes painful memories to be read by people you do not even know. Please know that by sharing your story and allowing yourself to be vulnerable you will help others to move past their own shame and guilt. You should be very proud of who you have become, and anytime you start to feel scared of judgment please pull your mind back to God's perfect love. Also, please know that because you have encountered God's patience, grace, and anointing that you will now be able to offer the same to others.

In sharing your story you have set the stage for change, not only in yourself but in others as well. Know that your testimony is not your own but God's, for he uses you to tell a story that is both powerful and beautiful. Please never forget what a beautiful, courageous, and strong woman you are and that your past never defines you. Who you are is greater than drug or sex addiction, your deepest darkest secrets, and your perceived shortcomings. You are a child of God. I hope that you continue to grow in Christ and continue to aim to live and love as Jesus did. Always be proud of your willingness to follow your small, still voice, and know that there is always a higher power guiding and governing your every thought.

Remember that God always turns everything around for good. Keep your heart open and mind quiet as you move forward thorough life. God cannot work with a closed heart. Always follow your heart and dreams, even if it seems crazy to everyone else. Trust in God's wonder-working power and know deep in your being that you are right on track. Continue to take risks and keep love at the forefront of your life. Never be ashamed of where you've been or what you've felt compelled to share, or not share, with the world. The right people will use your story to inspire and grow in love. The rest might not be ready, and that's okay. Know that you are perfect the way you are, and God is and will always be in control.

Go ahead with love and take pride in your ability to assess and release your attachments. Go forward with kindness and humility, yet never apologize for the decisions you've made. Stand in power with God and know that both your relationship with God and your spiritual journey are highly personal. You owe no explanations for any choices you've made, and no one else owes you that either.

Let go of anger and resentment. Forgive others and choose compassion over anything else. Choose to maintain an attitude of worship and gentleness, and observe more than you speak. Ask yourself difficult questions and always be comfortable with what makes you uncomfortable, it is only showing you where there's work left to do. See beauty in your suffering and pull the grace from even the most difficult situations. Lastly, always know that you must put loving yourself first. You cannot rely on anyone to love you the way you will when you see God within you. Always be patient with yourself. Never, ever be afraid of change.

Love,

Jade Black

PS: You are always enough.

Spend copious amounts of time in mindful meditation.
Sit with the self.
Yes, this way
when the silence comes.
This way when you struggle to move you'll be prepared,
whispering to yourself,
"Never forced am I, for I've known you all along."